BAD MEXICAN,
BAD AMERICAN

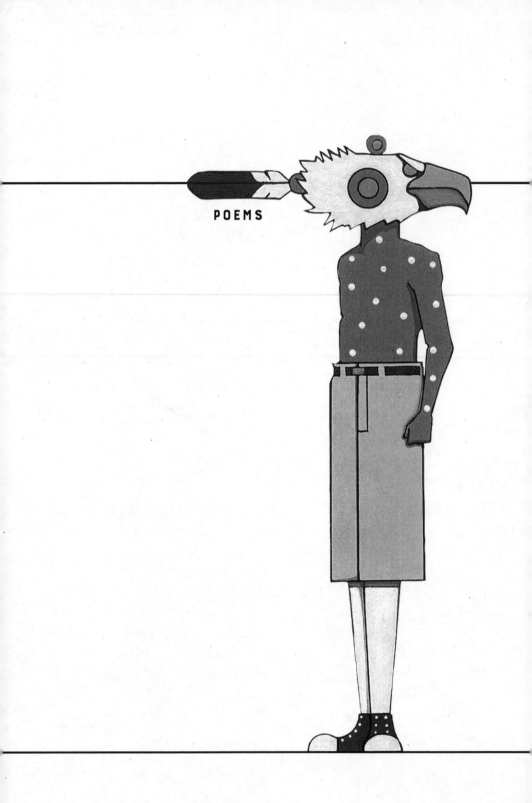

POEMS

BAD MEXICAN,
BAD AMERICAN

JOSE HERNANDEZ DIAZ

ACRE

CINCINNATI 2024

Acre Books is made possible by the support of the Robert and Adele Schiff Foundation
and the Department of English at the University of Cincinnati.

ISBN-13 (pbk) 978-1-946724-73-1
ISBN-13 (ebook) 978-1-946724-74-8

Designed by Barbara Neely Bourgoyne
Cover art: *Spotted Vato* by Jamie Chavez. Acrylic on 16 x 20 wood panel. Reproduced
with permission of the artist.

The press is based at the University of Cincinnati, Department of English, Arts & Sciences
Hall, Room 248, PO Box 210069, Cincinnati, OH, 45221-0069.

Acre Books books may be purchased at a discount for educational use. For information
please email business@acre-books.com.

For my parents, Maria and Esteban Hernández.

For my high school English teacher, Mrs. Kimberly Weir.

CONTENTS

III

IV

BALLAD OF THE WEST COAST MEXICAN AMERICAN/CHICANX

> Arboles de la barranca
> ¿Por qué no han enverdecido?
> Es que no los han regado
> Con agua del rio florido
> Me puse a amar a una mujer
> Con la ilusión de amar. . . .
>   —Mexican ranchera

My American friends think I'm too Mexican.
My Mexican friends think I'm too American.
My Mexican American friends are my road dogs.

Mi gusto es escribir poesía toda la noche
y toda la mañana.
Mi gusto es escribir poesía toda la noche
y toda la mañana.

I don't like my chile too hot; I like it just right.
I don't like my chile too hot; I like it just right.

When I'm drinking on the weekend,
And I play "Arboles de la Barranca,"
It doesn't matter who's singing it,
I feel 100% Mexican—those trumpets, damn.

I put ketchup in my breakfast burrito;
I put ketchup in my breakfast burrito:

Con la ilusión de amar.

DOÑA OFELIA

My cousin Jesús, "Jesse" as we grew up calling him,
asks if I can go with him to LAX to get his grandmother, Doña Ofelia.

He picks me up at 9 p.m. in his old-school '93 Buick Park Ave.
Along the drive, he plays old-school Easy-E and reminisces

about the old days. I was still young in the early '90s
when gangster rap hit. He tells me rappers are also poets.

I tell him: "Every time someone tells me they don't like poetry,
I ask if they like rap? They say 'yes.' I tell them rap is poetry."

At the airport we park and get a wheelchair for Doña Ofelia.
We wait five minutes at the gate before she arrives from Léon.

An airline worker pushes her in a wheelchair,
and they transfer her to us. My cousin,

who has probably been in more fights than visits to church,
gives his abuelita about five kisses in a row.

He tells her he loves her, "La quiero mucho, abuelita!"
On the ride home, Jesse and Doña Ofelia

talk about the latest news in their family and in the pueblo,
but Doña Ofelia is careful not to offend anyone,

or get in people's business too much. In fact,
at one point, she tells my cousin, "Yo no sirvo para pelear, mijo."

I'm no good at fighting. At my cousin's house,
we guide Doña Ofelia to the kitchen,

where we have café with pan dulce,
and my cousins open the gifts from México,

mostly candies and more coffee. As we sit and chat,
my cousin tells his grandma that I'm a writer

and I can write her life story. She lets out a light laugh and says:
"Mi vida ya paso, mijo." My life has already passed, son.

My tía, however, tells me that back in their pueblo,
a rough part of town, Doña Ofelia is respected

by the locals. Almost daily, neighborhood kids
go to her house and ask for beans for their bolillos.

Doña Ofelia never turns down any kid asking for food.
When these kids go the US, they make money,

working tough jobs, and when they come back to visit,
they always pay respects or buy gifts for Doña Ofelia.

At the end of the night, after I've said "Buenas noches"
to Doña Ofelia and my cousins, I have a final cigarette

with Jesse. He tells me, again, how I should tell
his grandma's life story or maybe even his.

I say that all it takes is one moment, like the story
about the beans and the bolillo and the neighborhood kids,

to say something special about someone. As for Doña Ofelia,
I tell him, she is part of the old ways of México.

"We are lucky to have her," I say.

FAMILIA

after Ray Gonzalez

All my ancestors were poor and I
am like my ancestors. I don't talk

about my personal life much. Why
complain? I had a loving family who

took care of me. A roof over my head.
Beans and tortillas on the stove.

Sure, there were eight of us in two rooms,
but we had plenty of space for love and

quarrels, of course. My dad only wears
his sombrero and vaquero belt

on special occasions. But his kindness
is always on display. My mother is

like a leader of a religion. Charismatic,
hardworking, and devout. My siblings

all went to college, but we know that
true education lies in your roots.

My abuelos both worked in the fields.
My abuelas raised plentiful children.

When I visit México, I walk in the mercado.
When I visit México, I'm ever alone.

Our culture is a badge of pride.
Our culture, nuestra cultura, will never die.

ODE TO THE OVERLOOKED MINIMALIST PAINTING
IN THE GALLERY

The best art is that which is overlooked or underappreciated:
A minimalist painting that is thought to be simple or bland.

My father's callused hands, his broken English, his constant
Obsession with the English language, which he will never master.

Someone tagged me in a post today, on Twitter, thanking me for being
One of their three followers. Someone ran after a crowded bus

Because they were late for reasons beyond their control.
Most Black, Brown, poor kids in the hoods, barrios, and trailer parks

Are starting from behind their privileged neighbors in the suburbs.
Survival of the fittest? Protestant work ethic is not the same

As centuries of privilege. I had a reading two months ago in
Venice Beach with three attendees. One was my mother.

The other two were guitarists from a local strung-out band.
It was the most intimate conversation at a reading I've ever had.

So we drank all the wine I brought and read some poems.
I feel like autumn is the most beautiful season and I know

It's cliché for a poet to say so, but decay, abandonment,
They make us stronger, wiser, more human, if they don't kill us first.

ROOTS THAT CRACKED THE PAVEMENT

I was born in a small apartment with giant roots that cracked the pavement. We ate frijoles and tortillas every day, with rice and cheese, sometimes carne asada on birthdays or holidays. I grew up in a rough neighborhood of low-rent apartments, which was inside a larger good neighborhood with middle-class homes. I didn't notice this until we went to high school and most of the kids drove brand new cars and had new stylish clothes from the mall. I had some new clothes too but mostly a lot of hand-me-downs and clothes from garage sales. I drove a 1992 Chevrolet Corsica that had been defaced by rival gang members. No, I wasn't in a gang, never interested me, but my brother had borrowed the car; it's a long story. Anyway, this apartment I grew up in, it had giant brown roots that cracked the pavement, the pavement full of graffiti, with graffiti names like: Screwy, Dosic, Zoner, Chaos, Gato, all of these first-gen guys from the neighborhood growing up like me, between cultures, between poverty and wealth, trying to make a name for themselves, for the neighborhood.

MY FATHER NEVER ATE UNTIL EVERYONE HAD EATEN

It wasn't that bad. We had enough to eat. To get by.
Just barely, but our parents never really let us know

the depth of our struggle. They never complained about
sacrificing everything for their children. For a better life.

In fact, daily, Dad wouldn't eat at the table with us.
He would just say, "Ustedes comen, no tengo hambre."

I used to get mad at him for not eating with us. Everyone
I knew ate as a family. I didn't know we were just getting by.

All I wanted to do was watch the Lakers and Dodgers and football.
No, I didn't know he didn't join us at the table because he wanted

to make sure we all had enough to eat. Not just barely, until we were full.
Then he'd eat. I used to hate when he'd do that, because I wanted

to eat with my father at the head of the table. But now I know, I ate because
of my father's sacrifice, and there is nothing—no painting, or poem—

as beautiful as a father's ineffable love.

BROKEN

My father tells me we need to stop speaking Spanish.
>He says my Spanish is trash and we should focus on English.
>He says a doctor told him the problem with my bipolar
is due to the fact that English-only was not enforced in our home.

>I know my dad. No doctor told him that. He uses imaginary
conversations with doctors to legitimatize his points.
I tell my dad his English isn't perfect either. Better than your Spanish,
>he says. I laugh and laugh, but inside I am angry and hurt.

Yet I know my dad has a point and at the same time doesn't.
>He wants stability, not broken languages, which lead to broken homes.
>I feel like telling him, we come from broken people who build
themselves up. I feel like telling him the brokenness in my Spanish,

>like the brokenness in his English, is part of who we are,
like it or not. Sure, we can try to improve it, but we have
nothing to prove. I feel like telling my father all of this,
>but instead, I put the Laker game on louder: *What's the score, anyway?*

MY MOTHER'S "BROKEN" ENGLISH

Is more beautiful than a Neruda poem.
Is always managing to get by.
Is lovelier than a spring rose garden.
Will comfort you like a sarape.
Is not afraid of the dark.
Is commanding yet vulnerable.
Can calm me down or lift me up.
Can handle doctor visits and bureaucratic phone calls.
Has taught me how to read poetry.
Has become masterful over the years.
Sounds magical in prayer.
Sounds magical in prayer.

THE POCHA WITH THE ADELITA TATTOO

I fell in love with the Pocha with the Adelita tattoo.
She's so cultured and idiosyncratic. Her hair is up in a bun.

She wears heels with blue jeans. Red lipstick.
Her tattoo is Day of the Dead and Mexican Revolutionary themed.

Her eyes are Pocha light brown, like honey.
I don't know if she speaks Spanish. If she does,

it's probably broken, like mine. The Pocha with an Adelita tattoo
and I go out on a date to a local taco shop. We talk about music,

art, and poetry. We have a few cocktails and eat tacos.
At the end of the night, I ask her about her tattoo.

She says she got it because it represents her Mexican heritage
and because Las Adelitas were "badass women."

I tell her it's lovely and lean in for a kiss.

EL CHACAL

Growing up in the neighborhood, everyone called me The Jackal or El Chacal. It was a term of endearment. At least, I think so. I was rather slick, like a jackal in the moonlight. A wise guy in the sense that I read philosophy books I didn't understand. I could handle my beer, that was my true talent. When I was younger, I ran with the wrong crowd, but everyone has since grown up and become family folks. I have a tattoo of a jackal on my bicep. It is rather gothic looking. I think people called me jackal because I'm up-front yet undersized. Maybe it's actually just because I have funny pointed ears. When I wrote graffiti back in the day, I only wrote in Spanish: El Chacal. I'd also draw the outline of a jackal's head with the tag. I've since branched out to tattooing folks and experimenting with canvas painting. I'll always remember those days in the neighborhood, though, as special to me. I get the urge to tag my name on a blank wall, again, every now and then. But I know I can't go back to my youth. I can only remember it with a beer or a glass of wine or a painting. Right now, I'm thinking of painting a ghost in a rearview mirror.

FOLK SONG

A man in a Las Cafeteras shirt sang along to Ramón Ayala. It was late winter. He drank from his Cerveza Bohemia. The man in a Las Cafeteras shirt was a Pocho, so his Spanish was somewhat broken, but when he sang along to Ramón Ayala, his voice was beautiful. The man listened to Ramón Ayala on YouTube. Originally, he started listening to Ramón Ayala from hanging out with his primos. The man wasn't even sure if Ramón Ayala had written the songs himself or perhaps they were passed down from generation to generation. The man in a Las Cafeteras shirt felt like a regular macho when he sang. At once brave and stoic; at once romantic and chivalrous. The man in a Las Cafeteras shirt felt like he could suddenly ride a horse. In fact, when he'd visited Michoacán as a young man, he once rode a horse with a cerveza in hand. He wasn't really a macho, though, even though he was good at football in high school. He was somewhere in the middle: between softie and macho. For now, though, as he listened to Ramón Ayala belt out another ranchera classic, the man in a Las Cafeteras shirt took a final sip of his Cerveza Bohemia and called it a night.

BILDUNGSROMAN OF A DISADVANTAGED BROWN KID

You were more of an observer than a participant.
    You knew right from wrong but didn't always do right.
You had less than others did but more natural gifts.

    Your parents sacrificed a lot for you to be a late bloomer.
It didn't rain much in childhood but that's not saying much.
    Sometimes, you'd come home after sunset, but you were just playing ball.

Some of your friends and siblings took fateful, wrong turns.
    But you're still alive and you've no fear of tomorrow.
You're still alive and statistics mean nothing to you.

You're still alive with a flame in your hand.

I NEVER HAD A MEXICAN AMERICAN TEACHER GROWING UP

Or any teacher that wasn't white. Just stating
    some facts. In fact, my teachers were wonderful, white as

    they were. I lived in a multicultural neighborhood,
but it took longer for that to be reflected in our educators.

    Today, I hope, it's much more diverse.
I guess that's part of the reason why I don't feel comfortable

as a teacher. Never seen a Mexican male English teacher.
    Also, however, I think I would find

any excuse not to stand in front of a group of strangers.
    My therapist tells me maybe I can be that teacher one day,

    for someone else. That Brown teacher talking about poetry.
Comparing a father's hands to battlefields and strawberry fields.

    Maybe I could be that teacher, one day, today, perhaps,
who teaches a Brown boy how to sing in verse, and in stories.

LA PALETA

A man in a Rage Against the Machine shirt went to the market to buy a Michoacána popsicle. It was his favorite popsicle. The flavor he got was fresa, or strawberry. He purchased the popsicle and then went to his job interview. He was applying to be a professor. He'd never had a Mexican American or Latinx teacher growing up in K–12, but he had some inspirational professors in college. During the interview, the man in a Rage Against the Machine shirt was asked about his shirt: "Why are you wearing a Rage Against the Machine shirt to an interview?" "Rage got me into poetry," the man said. "If it weren't for Rage and a few influential teachers, I never would've pursued literature." "Very nice," said the interviewer. The next week, the man received an email. He would be teaching The Writing of Contemporary Poetry at his local community college. On the first day of class, he picked a Michoacána popsicle as a starting point for a writing assignment. The students wrote poems and stories.

MY NAME

My name is very plain, Jose Hernandez.
I used to go by Joey Hernandez growing up.

I never asked anyone to call me that.
It was just a nickname. I always wrote Jose Hernandez

on my schoolwork. My teachers called me Jose.
However, all my friends and family called me Joey.

Some people still call me that. I don't mind it.
I always wanted an American name, growing up,

like my Pocho friends, Anthony, Jon, and Michael.
It's not so much that I was a sellout. I just wanted

to fit in. Blend in with the background. Not stand out
so much. When I first heard the names of the band members

of At the Drive-In, and the fact that they used the Spanish custom
of both the father and mother's surnames, I knew I wanted

to do the same. I changed my Myspace name.
I felt unique and cultured. Then, in college at UC Berkeley,

I read Gabriel García Márquez and it was confirmed:
From then on, I became Jose Hernandez Diaz. For a while,

I even used accent marks, thinking I was keeping it even more real.
Some people pronounce my name in Spanish. I don't mind it,

of course. Both are my real name.

THE SKELETON AND THE PYRAMID

A skeleton with a sombrero sat on top of an Aztec pyramid. The sun was setting. He played a song on his old guitar; it was called "The Jaguar Moon." At the end of the song, he took a bow for the small crowd that had gathered. The tourists clapped and tipped the skeleton plenty of pesos. The skeleton climbed down from the pyramid and bought a paleta de coco. It was his favorite flavor since childhood. The moon rose like a child's rainbow kite. Eventually, the skeleton finished the paleta and disappeared into the crowd of restless tourists.

BAD MEXICAN, BAD AMERICAN

I like football, ketchup on my scrambled eggs;
    My biggest sin, perhaps, is I speak English to my parents.

I'm a bad Mexican. Yet I like carne asada over BBQ,
    Latina women who speak Spanish in my ear.

I root for México in soccer. I'm a bad American too.
    I like Sunday morning rain. Winter holidays.

I've found solace in the jaded moon. Not everything is this,
    Or that. I once spelled my name as "Joey."

Was born in a racist nation. Not a troublemaker, just call it
    Like I see it. My patriotism: red, white, and blue. I've got

Two tattoos on my chest: a Mexican flag, and American too.
    My children will likely speak less Spanish than me.

Does that make you happy? I'm trying to do better: leyendo
    Poesía por la noche. Fusion is more than a cable channel in my barrio.

It was said before me, it will be said after: how you treat
    Folks is all that matters, to the dying question:

How do you want to be remembered?

THE MAGICIAN

A magician went to the market. He wore a scarf and sunglasses so the townspeople might not notice him. He got eggs and milk. He got toilet paper. As he was examining the apples, a young lady spotted him. "You're the magician, aren't you?! You're Carlos, The Magician!" "Yes, I'm The Magician," he said. "But I'd really just like to buy some fruit." The lady went on and on to Carlos about how she loved his shows, his wand, his illusions. How he could make a giant pickup truck disappear. "Thank you, kindly," said Carlos. He politely shook the lady's hand and went to pay for his items. He checked out, this time without any detection, and drove home.

As he drove home, he noticed a pair of jokers in the street. They began to fistfight. It started to rain. The jokers rolled around the pavement like dogs in the rain. The magician then pulled his car over, exited the vehicle, and calmly walked up to the jokers. "Abracadabra!" the magician shouted as he waved his wand. In the blink of an eye, the jokers transformed into a pile of tulips. Red tulips. Yellow tulips. Black tulips. The magician got in his car and drove home. It was the beginning of spring.

THE SURREALIST CAFÉ

A man in a Santa on a Surfboard shirt walked by a café. It was called The Surrealist Café of Southern California. He went inside. Sitting there were Salvador Dalí and Guillaume Apollinaire. The man in a Santa on a Surfboard shirt ordered three coffees, for all of them, plain but with a little bit of sugar. They thanked him. The three men discussed politics, at first, but then naturally began to tell jokes about the weather. "It is so cold, my moustache feels like a snowman's," said Dalí. They laughed. "It is so cold, my poems and philosophy seem upbeat and cheery," said Apollinaire. Then Pierre Reverdy walked in. Everyone shook his hand and they ordered him a plain coffee too. Reverdy quickly mentioned he wasn't in the mood for jokes. People were dying outside in the rain and all he wanted was a cigarette.

THE RECLUSE

A writing residency, at my kitchen table, where I wake up at 4 a.m. because of insomnia from meds and write a poem about a skeleton in a maze, and no one is around to say it's cliché, so I publish it in a book called *One Hundred Days of a Recluse*.

QUETZALCOATL IN THE CITY

I saw Quetzalcoatl at Panda Express in the city. I assumed he would strictly visit Mexican joints, but I'm sure he just wants variety, like anyone else. Quetzalcoatl ordered the "impossible orange chicken" bowl. I had no idea he's a vegetarian. Quetzalcoatl had on an elaborate, colorful headdress and carried a shield and a spear. I felt senselessly underdressed. I was in my flip-flops and a surfing shirt. I thought about going up and saying hello, but honestly, he was intimidating. Aztec God that he is. After Quetzalcoatl received his order, he tipped the workers, waved goodbye, and flew out the door. I ended up ordering the regular orange chicken with brown rice and vegetables. I ate there and then drove home at sunset.

INSOMNIAC MOON

A man couldn't sleep so he went outside to shout at the moon. "Damn you, moon! You're too bright! I can't sleep with that nonsense of yours!" Then the moon responded, "Well, I'm just doing what I'm meant to do. Shining. Avoiding complete darkness. Nothing would function without me." "Well, can you at least move west? I'd like a break, please," said the man who couldn't sleep. "I have an idea," said the moon. "Cover your head in your pillow and listen to classical music. You'll be asleep in no time." "That's actually not a bad idea!" said the man, excitedly. He ran upstairs, into his room, and covered himself with his pillow. He played Beethoven's Symphony No. 7. In a matter of minutes, he fell asleep. The moon, too, eventually disappeared.

THE GOLDEN TELESCOPE

I found a nineteenth-century golden telescope in the attic of an old house I bought to fix up. The house was located downtown, by the lake. The golden telescope was covered in an old cardboard box with spiderwebs. Written on the box was the phrase "The Stars Are Only the Beginning of Our Love."

I dusted off the telescope and brought it into the yard to look at the sky. To my surprise, I saw a pair of ghosts floating, dancing, really, in the autumn air. The ghosts were dressed in formal ballroom attire, the stars at their back. They appeared to be sipping martinis. I was shocked, so I sat down on the porch for a few minutes. This was going to be a hell of a place to live once I fixed it up, I thought. I would have to make a rooftop patio for the golden telescope, I decided. Everything else was secondary.

MIRAGE

A man walked in a desert on a Sunday afternoon. It was his birthday. He'd spent the morning walking in the desert after his horse died. The man was starting to feel weaker by the minute. Then he began to see a mirage: it was his fifth-grade teacher, Mrs. Cranford. Mrs. Cranford had died ten years ago. The mirage, or Mrs. Cranford, implored him to keep pushing, despite the oppressive heat of the desert. The man leaned toward the mirage, to give it a hug. It disappeared. The man looked up at the sky: the stars were beginning to shine.

NO INTERNET

A man didn't have internet on his computer. He didn't know what to do, so he turned on the television. He had bad reception. He adjusted the antenna. Nothing. So he decided to climb a mountain instead. He packed a backpack full of supplies and headed to the edge of the continent.

He struggled to climb the mountain at first but eventually made progress, little by little. The mountain was called Point Paz. When he finally got to the top of the mountain, he took a photo for Instagram. He raised his fist in the air and shouted, "I don't have the internet right now!"

THE HUMMINGBIRD GRAFFITI

A man was stuck on the Metro. It was autumn. Leaves fell from the trees onto the train on the tracks. The train was stuck between skyscrapers and a park. While the train was immobile, a graffiti artist walked up to the train with an LA Dodgers hat over his eyes. He painted a blue hummingbird on the train and then walked away. Within a few seconds, the train started running again. The people on the train clapped and then went back to their phones. The autumn wind was pleasant as the sun rose over the city.

LIZARD MAN

Although my body is that of a human, I have the head of a lizard. My lizard tongue is something of a show for people, but I've learned to embrace it. I rather like having a lizard head. Something different. Going against the mainstream. I listen to punk rock music, so it fits the aesthetic. I work as an art teacher, online. When the students first see me, they are polite for the most part. But I hear the whispers and giggles in the background. Can't deny it doesn't hurt a little. But pain makes you stronger. The best part about having a lizard head is the superior vision. I can see all the beauty in the details; lilacs blooming in the spring.

WOLVERINE ON HOLLYWOOD BLVD.

I wake up at 5 a.m. every day because I want to get ahead in life. I take a shower; fifteen minutes. I have breakfast and a coffee. I put on my Wolverine mask and go to Hollywood Blvd. By the time I get to the tourist section, I am already in character, both physically and psychologically. I charge $50 per photo to tourists. Everyone loves Wolverine. Spiderman is a wuss. Kind of a wacko, if you ask me. I think he's hooked on drugs, if I'm being real. Anyway, I wish him the best. No, I don't perform on the street. I don't dance. I just walk around like a badass. People gravitate toward me. I make a decent, honest living. At the end of the night, around 10 p.m., I drive on the cold freeway, still in uniform; still alive.

MY LIFE AS A FRENCH EXISTENTIAL NOVELIST

After I fell down the stairs last Easter, I was suddenly able to speak French. I moved to Paris immediately. I got a job at an old bookstore that Apollinaire used to frequent. I bought a French bulldog, of course. On the weekends I smoked too many cigarettes and rode the subway, aimlessly. My French name was Gaston, like in *Beauty and the Beast*, except I had no Belle. I'd always wanted to be a French Existentialist; now that I was one, I refused to wear a beret or the color black. My fatal flaw is that I think people are always looking at me; in fact, it's just that I was born a handsome child. Still, the moon shines more beautifully in Paris, France. The clouds, more beautiful.

THE ROAD

I was lost somewhere in the Bay Area, and I saw a sign that said, "Take This Road." I took the road straight ahead and didn't look back. After a couple of hours, I was in a land of nothing but my past and dreams. My deceased grandfather rode by on his mule on his way to work the fields. I saw Chick Hearn calling a basketball game between two of my friends who passed away from drugs. I kept driving. Next, I saw my elementary school teacher, Mrs. Cranford, baking banana nut bread on Christmas Eve. I wanted to try the bread, it smelled so good, but I didn't want to get out of the car because I thought I might disappear. Later, I saw some dinosaurs up ahead and I knew it was time to stop. I sat in the car until my dreams consumed me. I was never even born.

MEETING OCTAVIO PAZ ON THE PLANET JUPITER

I met Octavio Paz on the planet Jupiter last fall. He said he'd been living there since his death. Myself, I was on vacation with my family. When I first saw Paz, I paused and asked myself, "Should I go up to him? He's won the Nobel Prize." I did. I introduced myself as a comic book writer and illustrator and said that it was a pleasure to meet him. We shook hands. I didn't want to talk about writing with him, so I asked his favorite soccer team. "Pumas," he said. Later, he asked me the name of my most famous comic book so he could get a copy. "The Magician," I told him. It was getting cold on Jupiter, so we called it a night after that. I never forgot his calmness, though, his class and elegance.

MY DATE WITH FRIDA KAHLO

I went on a date with Frida Kahlo. Frida was like a mother to me or a muse at least, so it was kind of awkward at first. She sure was beautiful, though. She had on a colorful rebozo and one of her monkeys sat on her shoulder the entire date. I didn't mind, of course. Anything to sit next to Frida. In fact, I became close friends with the monkey. His name was "El Jaguar."

Anyway, Frida and I ate at an underground México City café. It was where real artists hung out. I felt out of place, but then again, she invited me there, so maybe I belonged. Frida and I had Cuban coffee and then vegetarian tacos. We sipped on mescal and black tea. At the end of the night, following an awkward silence during a conversation on Cubism, we kissed for about thirty minutes beneath a protest mural by David Alfaro Siqueiros. She asked to paint me, naked. I was too shy and refused. On the second date, she stood me up. I mourned for a couple of weeks and then moved on to my irrational pursuit of Rosario Castellanos.

MEETING JAMES TATE IN HEAVEN

I met James Tate at a carnival in heaven. Tate was riding the bumper cars
with his cat, Lucy. I was smoking a cigarette on the Ferris wheel with my dog,
incidentally named Carnival. We met in line to buy hot dogs. "My name is
Jose," I said. "I'm James Tate. Nice to meet you," he said. We ate our hot dogs
at a bench with graffiti scribbled by fallen angels. Tate asked me a couple
of questions: "What's your favorite season?" "Autumn," I said. "Who's your
favorite baseball team?" "The Dodgers," I said. "I like the Kansas City Royals,
myself," he said. As the clouds darkened and the carnival ended, the jugglers
and clowns packed up for the next town in heaven. Tate and I shook hands,
said our goodbye, and went our separate ways. Tate, to a fancy cocktail party
with the original nine muses. Myself, I went to a library of forgotten saints
on the other side of heaven.

THE JAGUAR TATTOO

A man in a Rage Against the Machine shirt chased a jaguar into the jungle. It wasn't that the jaguar feared the man, it was just tired and wanted to rest. The man wanted to get closer to his roots. He knew the jaguar was sacred to the Mayans. The jaguar jumped into a tree. It began to rain. The man sat beneath the tree and started drawing the jaguar onto his sketchbook. It was a fine sketch, for sure.

Later, when he arrived back in the suburbs of Los Angeles, the man in a Rage Against the Machine shirt got a tattoo of the jaguar in the tree. He wondered if it was cliché for a Pocho to get a tattoo of a jaguar; he didn't care, though. In fact, whenever he drank enough whiskey, he'd tell the story of chasing a jaguar into the jungle on a summer afternoon. He'd even make up a part about wrestling with the ancient beast—and winning.

THE ROOSTER TATTOO

A man in a Chicano Batman shirt got a rooster tattooed onto his shoulder. The rooster was bright orange, like a mango. It was postmodern colors, he told everyone. The man didn't feel much pain as he got the tattoo. He also had a jaguar on his forearm and a snake on his back.

When he showed the rooster tattoo to his girlfriend, she immediately said it was beautiful, "muy bonito." They made love that night. Later that week, he thought about his next tattoo, perhaps a mariachi and a guitar, he told his girlfriend. She agreed. They made love, again. That night, he had the same recurring dream he'd been having for weeks: it was a dream about a rooster on a farm, in their family's rancho, back in México.

THE SHOWDOWN

A man in a Rage Against the Machine shirt overthrew the government—of his house. Moreover, he successfully defeated his wife and three-year-old daughter in an argument about what to watch on television. The wife and child wanted to watch *Frozen* for the seventy-seventh time. The Man in a Rage Against the Machine shirt wanted to watch the Dodgers game.

They decided to play rock, paper, scissors. The man faced his child. He drew rock. She drew scissors. The man jumped up and down. "Victory! Sweet victory," he shouted. When the Dodgers game was over, the man swept the kitchen, mopped, and threw out the trash. His wife and child had fallen asleep thirty minutes earlier in another room watching Elsa do princess things.

THE VOID

A man in a Pink Floyd shirt drank a bottle of champagne. He had just won a major literary prize. The prize was called The Void Is Real Prize. It was awarded to the writer with the biggest void. The man in a Pink Floyd shirt toasted with a group of imaginary friends: Cheers to void. Cheers to clouds. Cheers to the moon. Cheers to autumn's leaves. He drank and drank. Then he fell to the floor. He wrote a poem on the floor. It was a sestina, but he didn't know it was a sestina. He was born on the Fourth of July. No one cared. But he'd just won a major literary prize. The Void Is Real Prize of 2020.

THE ANARCHY

A man in a Pink Floyd shirt rode a horse on the sand at the beach. He wasn't on a date. He was alone with nature. The waves splashed in the background. A surfer waved at him. He waved back. Then the horse started charging. It charged at a dragon who was getting ready to douse the pier in flames. The man in a Pink Floyd shirt pulled out his slingshot and fired magical stones at the dragon. The dragon managed to dodge the stones but asked for peace. They shook on it. The dragon now lives on the coast by the pier and is retired from causing anarchy. In fact, the man in a Pink Floyd shirt and the dragon often ride motorcycles together on the weekend. There is still a mild anarchy as they ride, but it has been significantly subdued.

THE FAIR

A man in a Pink Floyd shirt rode the Ferris wheel at the local fair. He smoked a cigarette as he went around in circles. He saw the pier in the distance. He dreamed of learning to surf. *Maybe next weekend*, he thought. He continued smoking as he went around in circles. No one else was on the ride. It was a Wednesday afternoon.

The man in a Pink Floyd shirt eventually got off the ride. He then went on the bumper cars. He played the ring toss even though he thought it was probably a scam. He won a giant neon-pink teddy bear! He had a great time, overall. At sunset, he pulled out a notebook and wrote his recently deceased mother a letter:

Dear mother, I miss the times we spent together laughing, fighting, singing, but most of all, I miss the times we spent at the fair. I am here tonight alone. I won a giant teddy bear. I will take it to your grave tomorrow morning. Te quiero mucho, The Man in a Pink Floyd Shirt.

EL MELANCÓLICO

A man in a Chicano Batman shirt rode his lowrider bicycle in the sunshine. It was still technically winter, but in the afternoon, there was plenty of sunshine: it was southern California. The man in a Chicano Batman shirt arrived at the library. He checked out Baudelaire's *Paris Spleen*. Baudelaire was his favorite writer, even though he thought the Frenchman was a little crazy. "Life is kind of crazy," the man in the Chicano Batman shirt said. After he checked out the book, he went home and read it. There was graffiti written on the walls and sewers of his barrio; not a lot, but enough to scare the white people away. When the man arrived in his apartment, he made a strong coffee and began flipping through the book. His favorite prose poem was "The Old Clown." Then, "The Stranger." "That Baudelaire was one melancholy fuck," the man in a Chicano Batman shirt said; "just like me."

THE PIRATE SHIP

A man in a Chicano Batman shirt scuba dove at the bottom of the ocean. It was late summer. He saw an old turtle covered in algae swimming by slowly. He saw a school of viperfish. He saw tons of interesting rocks but also debris. Then he discovered a pirate ship. It looked like it was from the seventeenth century. He swam toward the ship. On the ship, he found a skeleton captain floating in the bridge. The skeleton captain still had on a pirate hat, and his sword was attached to his belt. The man in a Chicano Batman shirt was shocked but also excited. He dug into the skeleton captain's pockets in search of gold. He found two gold coins. Written on the gold coins was the phrase "Life is a Voyage."

The man in a Chicano Batman shirt grabbed the coins and swam to shore. He got dressed and headed to the local town square. When he got to the town square, he took the coins to a fountain in the center of the square. He threw the coins in the fountain and said a prayer to himself, "I pray for my band to make it big, but in an honest way. I pray for adventure like the pirates, but without their demise. I pray for a ship, an ocean, and a sun that doesn't set."

THE FALL

A man in a Chicano Batman shirt fell from a skyscraper. He didn't have a
parachute on. He did have on a pair of parachute pants, though. He couldn't
fly, but he was able to break-dance in the air, as he descended on the city:
he was fly! He showed off some fancy footwork. He did a headstand in
midair and spun around in circles. As he prepared to land, a fireman threw
a trampoline on the sidewalk. The man in a Chicano Batman shirt bounced
around the city. As he landed, he did the splits. The crowd cheered. He took
a bow and waved at the many faces in the city.

THE OLLIE

A man in a Chicano Batman shirt skated along the border. He was going back to the US. Instead of waiting in line, he ollied over the border wall. As he landed, he crossed himself.

Then he went to Alberto's Tacos. He ordered a California Burrito. When he was in México that summer, he'd enjoyed plenty of authentic meals, but now that he was back in the states, he craved a Pocho classic: the California Burrito. Carne asada, fries, pico de gallo, sour cream, and a bit of salsa. He was set. It was delicious. When he finished, he rode to the bus station and headed back to southeast Los Angeles. It was the last day of winter.

ODE TO A CALIFORNIA NECK TATTOO

A man in a Chicano Batman shirt got a tattoo of the state of California on his neck. He rode his longboard to the tattoo parlor early in the morning. This was going to be his third tattoo. He also had a tattoo of palm trees on his chest and a skeleton on a surfboard on his calf. He smoked a cigarette as he arrived at the shop.

Everything went smoothly. It didn't hurt much. He was a little worried he might be perceived as a gangster, but he knew real gangsters could tell the difference between soldiers and civilians. He rode his longboard home. The sun peeked through the fog.

The man in a Chicano Batman shirt was born in southern California. He went to college in northern California. He'd never lived anywhere else. He didn't want to. Couldn't imagine living in a place that didn't have Mexican Americans. He wasn't arrogant about it. He just loved the sunshine and the ocean and the tacos and the murals to La Virgen de Guadalupe.

SUNDAY CRUISE

A man in a Chicano Batman shirt drove his 1972 Chevy Camaro down Beach Blvd. Sunday was the best day for cruising. It was the beginning of spring. There was still a slight chill in the air, but it was better than frigid winter. As the man in a Chicano Batman shirt approached the ocean at sunset, he began to play his "neo-soul" music louder. A few surfers still surfed in the background. Plenty of people lay on the sand with their towels and umbrellas to block the sun. As the man in a Chicano Batman shirt turned right on Bellflower Blvd., he left the beach and headed back to southeast Los Angeles. Sunday night was always smooth and mellow.

TUESDAY

A man in a Chicano Batman shirt rode a lowrider bicycle on the ocean waves. He was not on acid. He was not dreaming. He was actually riding a bicycle on the water. He is not Jesus. He is not a demon. He was literally pedaling on the sea. He is not a hologram. He is not a myth. He was definitely riding a bike on the ocean waves. It is not surreal. It is not a metaphor. I saw it. It really happened. It was on a Tuesday.

THE CONFORMIST

A man in a Neil Young & Crazy Horse shirt drank coffee at 4 a.m. because there was nothing else to do. He looked out the window: a pair of Doberman pinschers walked by in the moonlight. The man remembered his own Doberman pinscher from childhood. In retrospect, the dog was far too big and strong for a child. Sweet memories. The man finished his coffee and went to the gym. He walked on the treadmill for an hour, even though it bored him, immensely. The man in a Neil Young & Crazy Horse shirt was becoming more mature in life. Finally, he was getting better at doing things he didn't really like. When he finished at the gym, the man went home and watched American football and ate a turkey sandwich. He was conforming very well to society; he was living the dream.

THE REBEL

A man in a Mars Volta shirt fell off a skateboard. The city was essentially abandoned. There was a virus in town, but he insisted on skating. As soon as he fell off the board, he bounced back up. He was a loner, a misanthrope. He chain-smoked cigarettes, because he was young and foolish. He wore the same pair of pants every day. He hadn't had a girlfriend in six years. But he was very creative, a painter and poet. So creative, he often forgot to tie his own shoes. He was terrible at putting furniture together. They say when he stared women in the eyes, he was irresistible. Yet he was afraid of eye contact. I'd tell you more about the man in a Mars Volta shirt, but I need a cigarette. The world is ending; I don't want to waste it on poetry.

THE STRANGER

A man came up to me as I was walking home from the pharmacy, "Are you Jose Hernandez Diaz?" "Yes," I said, "who's asking?" "Do you enjoy sipping tea before bedtime?" "Well, I do, but what is it to you?" I asked. "In the ninth grade, did you get cut from the basketball team?" "I did, in fact, get cut from the team." "Do you sometimes wonder what life would've been like had you married Margot Cisneros?" "Maybe, sometimes, yes," I said. "Are you afraid of small talk and long walks in the city?" "I'm just a little introverted," I said. "Does the night sky resemble a dragon of your dreams?" "Yes, thank you for asking," I said. "Did you cry when Muncy hit that home run in the World Series?" "I did cry at that moment. Proud of it!" "Were you born and raised back and forth from LA to Orange County?" "Story of my life; yes," I said. "Does the night sky resemble a dragon of your dreams?" "Yes, thank you for asking. Yes!"

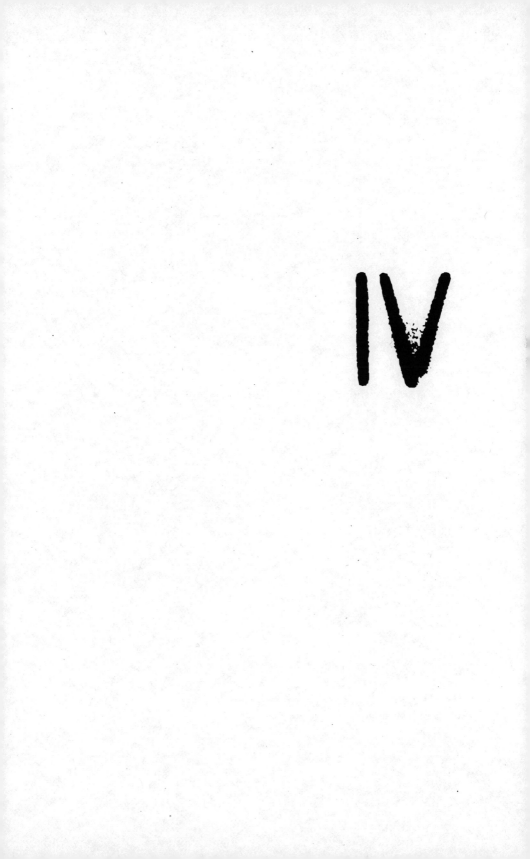

IV

VOICE

A man in a Carlos Santana shirt looked for his voice beneath a pile of crisp autumn leaves. Nothing. He looked for his voice at an underground rooster fight. Nothing. The man in a Carlos Santana shirt picked up a bulldog puppy and looked for his voice inside the dog's mouth. Nothing. Finally, the man in a Carlos Santana shirt saw a used black guitar in a thrift store window. He purchased the guitar with his last few dollars. The man tuned the guitar and began to play a bolero. His voice was there, as it turns out, inside of the guitar sound hole. It had been there all along.

THE MOON

My first day on the moon was a pleasant experience. I had been a political prisoner for a few months back home in a country I won't name. I was against the government in general. I didn't have a specific economic or social policy gripe; I just didn't like their bland uniforms and puppet shows. Their national anthem was a bit monotone and soulless. It lacked fine word choice, or nuance for that matter.

So, when I arrived on the moon as an exile, I welcomed the change. The prison was beginning to kill my spirit. On the moon I was free to do as I pleased. I mean, I had to wear a space suit and bounce around like a kangaroo, but I got used to it. You get used to things, as a man, you soldier on. The lack of food and water was initially problematic, but I began to realize that true nourishment came from the stars.

On my last day on the moon, I didn't realize it was going to be my last day. It rained peacock feathers as cotton candy clouds overflowed the atmosphere. Dolphins flew freely in the sky like doves in Renaissance paintings. I sat near a pair of dragons and played the harmonica. I was on the moon, but it felt like a silver dream. A dream where you can't wake up. I never did wake up, actually. It was the most peaceful sleep of my life.

THE GARGOYLE

A gargoyle arrived at my patio in autumn. It was made of charcoal granite. The gargoyle flapped its wings slowly as it landed on the pavement. I asked if it wanted some water. It shook its head no. I pulled out a cigarette and puffed away. I asked the gargoyle if it wanted a smoke. No, again. I looked at the sky and wondered where the gargoyle came from. He seemed to guess my confusion, and spoke, "My name is Samson; I'm from the fifteenth century." That's amazing!" I said. "What brings you to the suburbs of Los Angeles?" "I've been wanting to see the future. The modern world. I want to get a place out here in the suburbs. Away from the city," he said. "What city do you live in?" I asked. "I'm a Parisian, a Frenchman," he said. "Fascinating," I said, looking up at the sky. "How did you get here, anyway?" I asked. "It was a matter of wishing upon a blood moon. I made a wish to live in suburban Los Angeles in the year 2020," the gargoyle said. "That's amazing!" I said. "So, where do you recommend I go for quiet and darkness?" the gargoyle asked. "Well, this place is known for sunshine and palm trees. But if you find the right isolated spot along the coast, you'll have fog every morning, at least, and views of the vast ocean at night," I said. "Then the coast it is, friend. Thank you for your time!" the gargoyle said as he flew westward. I didn't know exactly what had just happened, but I had a newfound respect for gargoyles and fifteenth-century Gothic architecture in general. The reticence. The melancholia.

THE ADVERTISEMENTS

A man read a newspaper. He saw an ad for dog food: "Free dog food!" He read more: "But you have to bark like a dog!" Then he read another ad: "Free chicken sandwich!" He read on: "But you have to come dressed as a chicken!" The man kept reading: "Free ice cream! But you have to scream into a bucket of cream!" Fed up, the man decided to throw the paper away. Instead, he turned on the television. He saw an ad for roses: "Free roses! But you have to tell me that you love me." The man laughed out loud. "What a deal!" he said as he picked up the phone to call.

THE FIRST DAY OF AUTUMN

A man ran into a pile of leaves. It was the first day of autumn. Red leaves. yellow leaves. Orange leaves. Purple leaves. *But no blue leaves?* He filled his briefcase with leaves. He was late to work, so he darted to the subway. On the subway, he pulled out a yellow leaf, which was also a pen, and began to write a letter to his boss.

Dear Boss, I've brought some leaves on the subway and it is autumn. Dear Boss, please forgive my tardiness, for it is autumn. The man ran out of the subway and climbed the tall staircases into his office. He poured out the leaves onto his desk as he sang a song about autumn, "The leaves in autumn, oh the joy! / The leaves in autumn, I rejoice!"

THE WEST

The West has a seagull as President. The West bathes in the sun and the moonlight. The West skates and surfs and raps and cruises. The West flies a kite in spring. The West does not fear winter or Mexicans. The West eats a burrito for breakfast. The West has Korean BBQ for lunch. The West never forgives. Never forgets. The West will not go down without a fight. The West is strong. The West is light. The West can hold a thorn rose between her lips. The West, The West, The West.

THE BLUE HUMMINGBIRD

The blue hummingbird paints abstract paintings, with its wings, on the ceilings of governments. The blue hummingbird does not sleep at all nor does it dream. The blue hummingbird steals nectar from the heart of a lion. The blue hummingbird once flew over a parade of Eagle and Jaguar Knights. The blue hummingbird sings odes to California at the coolest of dawn. The blue hummingbird can see over the Golden Gate Bridge, through the fog in the city. The blue hummingbird has been alive for twenty-two million years and is thriving. *Dear blue hummingbird, please hum me to sleep.*

THE OCEAN IS NOT A CAPITALIST

The man who was not a capitalist sat by the ocean. It was 6 a.m. He was not a surfer anymore. He had given it up to focus on painting. He painted the ocean and the clouds. Sometimes he painted bridges. He once painted a toad on a lily pad. It was spring.

Eventually, the man left the beach. He went to the library and ate a muffin with a coffee. He was not a capitalist, but he had a few government dollars to buy the minimum. The man who was not a capitalist read three books at a time. One was about a war in Europe, many years ago. Another book was about a castle in Europe, long ago. The last book he read was about the ocean: it was called *The Ocean Is Not a Capitalist.*

THE SURFER AND THE JAGUAR

A surfer surfed in the ocean. It was the beginning of autumn. The word *poem* was written on the chest of his wet suit. He caught a few waves, but mostly he was just trying to enjoy another day on earth, in his fortieth year. After about two hours of surfing, he exited the water. He sat on the sand and took it all in.

Then a jaguar approached the shore. The jaguar walked slowly on the warm sand. Immediately, the man went back into the ocean. He hovered on his board about two hundred feet in. The jaguar walked by, peacefully, and didn't see the man on the board, in the ocean. As the sun set, the man exited the water again and rode home on his bicycle. What a relief, he thought.

As the moon rose above the West Coast, the jaguar returned to the jungle. It fell asleep in a cave. It was a cool autumn night.

THE END OF A DECADE

A man played a guitar along the ocean shore. It was the end of December. It was the end of a decade. A seagull landed at his side. The man sang a song about the growth of palm trees along the shore. The clouds darkened. It began to rain. The man put his guitar down in the sand and took off his shirt. He had a wet suit underneath.

He began to surf in the ocean. It was December 31, in fact. It was the last day of the decade. He had forgiven his enemies. Instead, he focused on celebrating his sobriety, family, and friends. He smiled as he surfed in the ocean until sunset.

BONES

A dead man sent two dozen burgundy roses to his wife on their wedding anniversary. He had been dead for more than three years. He missed her immensely from the grave. He didn't have an actual heart anymore, no, but that's when he realized love comes from the bones.

When the dead man's wife received the burgundy roses, she read the note carefully: "They say true love never dies. Here are two dozen burgundy roses from the grave to prove it. Love, Antonio."

The woman smelled the fresh roses and opened the living room curtains. The spring sunlight was intoxicating. She could feel her dead husband's pulse inside of her lungs.

GHOST

Someone broke into my house and discovered me writing at 3 a.m. at my desk. "What are you doing that for?" they asked. "I have no life, I guess," I said. "That's too bad," they said. "Why are you robbing my house?" I asked. "I'm short on cash at the moment," they said. "What if I give you some poems instead? Or a couple of haikus," I said. "I'll see my way out. Thank you!" the thief said. When the door closed behind them, I got up and made another strong coffee; I continued writing my memoir, tentatively titled *My Life as a Very Real Ghost*.

AT THE FUNERAL FOR VAN GOGH'S EAR

I'm at the funeral for van Gogh's ear. His ear lived a passionate, colorful life. Van Gogh's blood was not red, like mine or yours, no, it was blue. Blue like the midnight ocean, despite the darkness. Van Gogh's ear received marigolds at the decadent funeral. It was held at midnight, in secrecy. Several celebrities attended the funeral, including the nose of Pablo Picasso. I was only invited because I used to polish van Gogh's shoes as a young student. One winter day, van Gogh came to my shop complaining about his ear. He said it rang loudly. He said it cried at night. Van Gogh and his ear will always be remembered, starry night after starry night.

AT THE CEMETERY OF DEAD POETS

I was trapped in a graveyard of dead poets. I was technically trapped but didn't want to get out, anyway. First, I went to Rosario Castellanos's grave and paid my respects. I addressed her as mother in Spanish, Madre de la Poesía. Then I went to Octavio Paz's grave. I wrote a small poem on the grave for El Gigante of Mexican letters. It was a haiku and that's all I'll say about it. Next, I went to James Tate's grave. I placed some white roses on the gravestone and shed a few tears. I glanced at the sunset. I said thank you, told him I owed him lunch. Then, I went to Russell Edson's grave. I dropped off a comic book I'd written and illustrated for him. I poured out whiskey in the grass next to the grave. Lastly, I went to Marosa di Giorgio's grave by the entrance. I immediately turned into a yellow jackal in the moonlight. The new moon had cast a spell on the city.

ACKNOWLEDGMENTS

Grateful acknowledgment is made to the following literary journals where some of these poems first appeared, sometimes in different forms:

Acentos Review, Anomaly, Barrio Panther, The Boiler, Boulevard, Carve, Centaur, Chattahoochee Review, Cherry Tree, Chestnut Review, Chiricú Journal, The Common, Conduit, Crazyhorse, diode poetry journal, Grist, Guesthouse, Hex, Honey Literary, Huizache, Indianapolis Review, LaHave Review, The London Magazine, Moria, The Night Heron Barks, No Contact, Northwest Review, Okay Donkey, Pacifica Literary Review, Parentheses Journal, Passengers Journal, Pithead Chapel, Poet Lore, Poetry Northwest, Poets.org, *Porter House Review, Qu, The Rumpus, Salamander, Sierra Nevada Review, Sixth Finch, Southern Indiana Review, Southern Review, The Spectacle, Sundog Lit, Sycamore Review, Timber, Whale Road Review, Witness,* and *Yale Review*

"El Melancólico" appeared in *Odes to Our Undoing: Writers Reflecting on Crisis* (Risk Press 2022).

"The Showdown" appeared in the *Até Mais: Latinx Futurisms* anthology edited by Alan Chazaro, Malcolm Friend, and Kim Sousa (Deep Vellum 2023).

Thank you to my parents, Maria and Esteban Hernández, for all their sacrifices for my siblings and me. Anything I accomplish as a writer, editor, teacher is because of your example, dedication, and sacrifices. Thank you!

Thank you to my high school English teacher, Mrs. Kimberly Weir. Thank you for believing in me, especially when I didn't believe in myself. Thank you for inspiring me to become a writer. When times were hard, I always remembered your belief in me and it helped keep me going. Thank you!

Thank you to Mrs. Summer Howe Ugale. Thank you for stapling my essays to the wall of your classroom when I was a high school student. It really helped shape my confidence and belief in myself as a writer. I consider it my first publications!

Thank you to Lisa Ampleman and the Acre Books team, a dream press for me. Thank you for your professionalism and for valuing and respecting my words and art. The day I found out this book was accepted by Acre Books was one of the happiest moments of my life.

Thank you to #PoetryTwitter for the continued support. It means more than you know. Thank you to the editors who've published me in various literary magazines around the world. Thank you, dear poetry readers!